To You Love Me

Kara DeMaio

To You Love Me. Copyright © 2020 by Kara DeMaio. All rights reserved. Printed in the United States of America. No part of this book may be used or reproduced without written permission except in the case of brief quotations embodied in articles and reviews.

Illustration by Kara DeMaio
Editing by Krista Petrosoff

ISBN: 978-1-7358455-0-0 (pbk.)

For more information, visit LifeTranscribed.com

For my love...

*With you,
I am home.*

Table of Contents

Before

Down the rabbit hole	8
Resuscitation	11
The night is hungry	12
Unanswered questions	14
Into the shadows	17
Still learning	18

After

Blindfold	22
Glass house	25
Melting	26
The list	29
Lost and found	30
Fireworks	33
Put me out	34
Made for you	36
Full bloom	37
Balancing Act	38

Before

Down the rabbit hole

I am empty again and I wonder how long it'll be this way—
the hunger for something more
constantly gnawing at my insides.

This place feels hollow and heavy at the same time—
so much so that it becomes hard to breathe.

I'm tired of constantly fighting to
keep my head above water.
Sometimes it feels easier to simply stop and sink.

It calls out to me, especially at night in the dark
when the world has continued to turn without me.

I want to give in.
I want to let go.

Sometimes I want to just disappear—
even for a little while—
because I miss not feeling
and not caring
and floating away,
when time seemed to stop
and nothingness surrounded me.

I miss the moments when nothing mattered,
the endless night stretched out in front of me
and I didn't have to try to search for
what it is that I am so sad without.

Sometimes, *I miss giving in.*

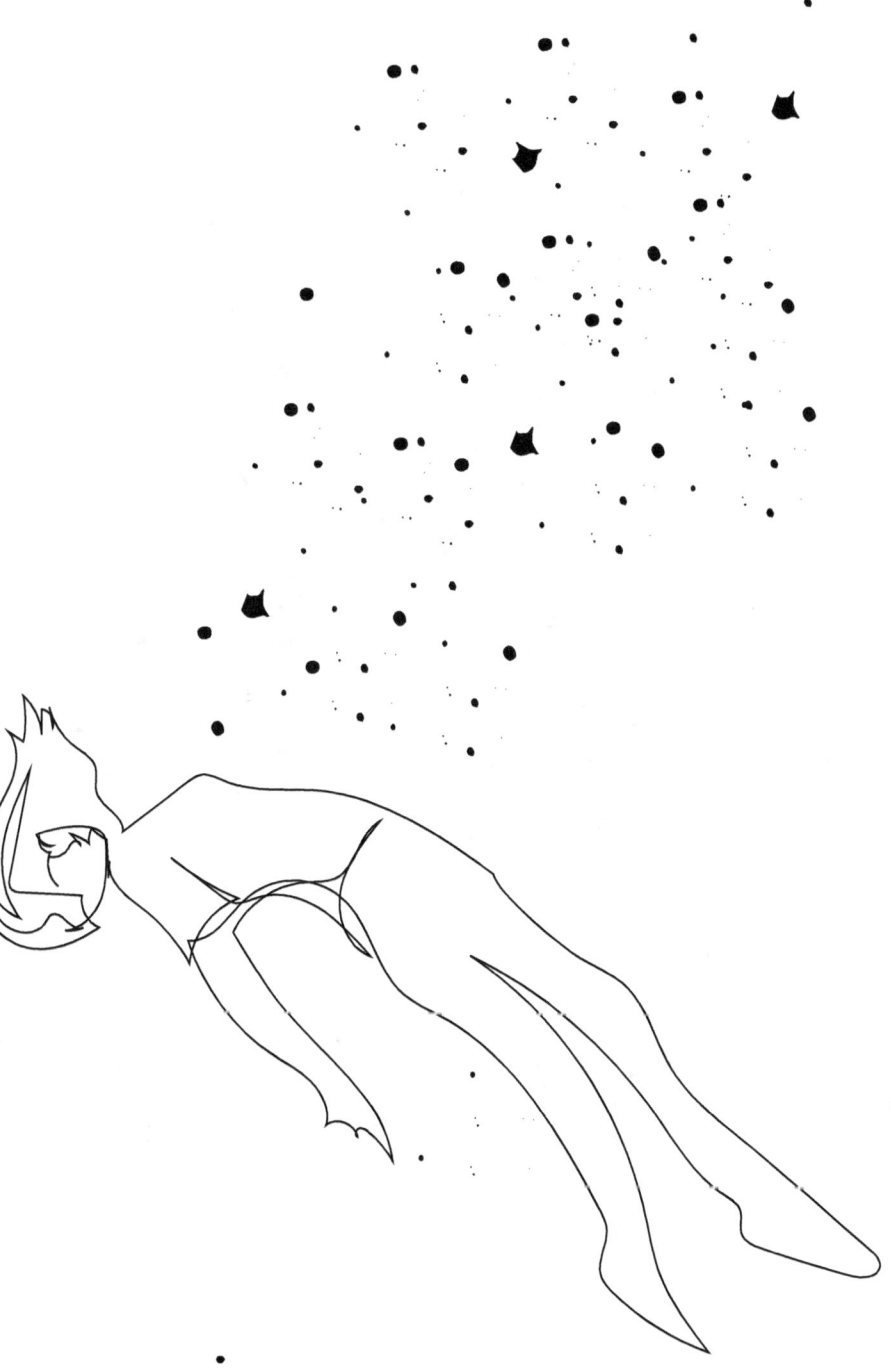

Resuscitation

Sometimes I cling to denial
so that reality won't drown me.

I'm lost in a world
where I don't feel so small,
helpless and unnecessary
like I do in this one.

I'm lost in a world
where loneliness doesn't
steal all of the air in the room
and I can be everything
I am supposed to be
without choking on the bitter taste of fear.

The night is hungry

I feel like I'm slipping away again-
little pieces drifting in the wind.

I worry that it's coming back,
but maybe it's been hiding all along.

I'm sliding backwards
down
    down
        down
a slippery slope
and I can't find a hold to grab onto.

Everything comes rushing back-
the fears that used to haunt me.

I can feel darkness creeping in at the edges so
I run as far and as fast as my legs can carry me.

Shadows are always lurking
and loneliness always threatens.
Angry voices fill my head-
taunting me with the past
and the way I used to speak to myself.

I want to escape the places that I've worked
so hard to get away from.
But it's there-always there-threatening at my heels.

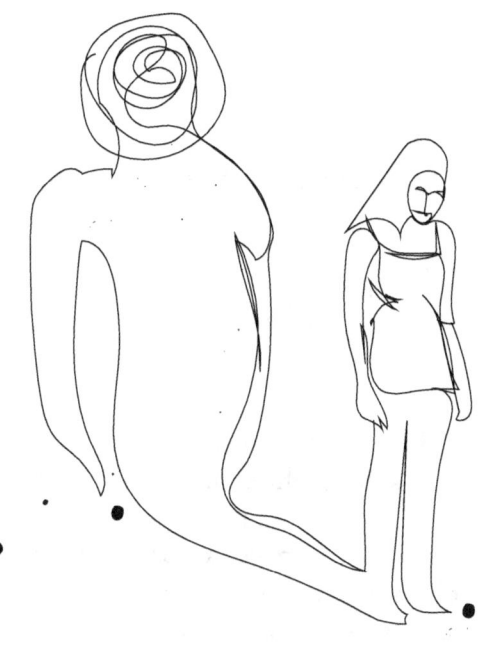

It never goes away.
It's a constant, never ending fight
that never lets up
and never lets me win.

I've never been one to choose the easy way out,
but sometimes temptation screams
louder than pride.

I want to portray strength,
but the truth is, I've always felt weak.

So I sit alone in silence
let the dark swallow me
until morning comes again.

Unanswered questions

I wonder how much you ever truly know someone
or if it's just what they let you see.

I wonder how much of our relationships through life
are based on real connections or
just what we want them to be.

I wonder how much damage we do to one another because
we can't love ourselves unconditionally.

I wonder sometimes
if love will run out
if I continue to give it away for free.

Into the shadows

Effortless and free—
all the things I'd love to be.

I watch the ease at which you speak,
laugh
play
smile
confront
the way your calm demeanor
spills over onto those around you,
putting them under your spell.

I disappear into the shadows behind you
where I've always been more comfortable
unsure if I put myself here or
if it's everyone else who does

I feel myself slip away, slowly
somewhat unnoticed by everyone else

I've lost what it feels like to be seen
I feel less—always less

It is so very exhausting—
the constant comparison—
and feeling like I never quite measure up.

Still learning

Sometimes I find myself alone among a room full of people.
I feel as though my soul will never connect with another
the way it has with you.
I wonder how it is that we are so connected and yet not,
so in sync and yet not,
meant for one another in some ways and yet not.

I'm still learning to stop chasing things not meant for me.
I'm still learning what it means to gracefully let go.
I'm still trying to figure out what it is that I want and
need and make my heart and mind agree on this.

I've never known what it feels like to give love to
and receive love from the same person,
but I'm tired of running away.
I'm tired of the chase.
I'm tired of games and dishonesty,
with ourselves and one another.
I'm tired of disappearing in the dark because it's
comfortable instead of being fearless in the light.

I'm tired of giving things up before they even begin.

I'm tired of going through every step of this life
without a hand to hold.

I want to spend my life with someone who thinks
it's possible to fall madly and hopelessly in love
and reminds me every day that it is.

After

Blindfold

They say that love makes you blind,
but I think people see what they want to see.
Traces of your fingertips across my skin
are memories fading into the night.

I fill my time so I'm not reminded
how empty being home feels-
how empty sleeping alone feels-
how alone I always seem to feel
despite all of the people who surround me.

I want to know what belonging feels like-
to have arms that hold me and make me feel at home.

Being in love and having someone love you-
it's a drug that takes over
making everything hazy and confusing.

You lose sight of the fact that it may be harming you
and you hold onto the high of it-
the feeling that makes your heart race.
But it's a vicious cycle when you come down from the high-
the earth crashing into you and walls closing in.

Every emotions feels tangled together-
excitement, fear, love, heartache, anticipation-
you can't pull one without getting them all.

I feel like I can't breathe,
or I won't breathe—
sometimes I have to remind myself to breathe.

I'm on a runaway train and I can't seem to get off,
but I don't want to be sidelined either,
watching the train leave me in its dust
filled with regret and unsure why.

I don't know where I'm heading—unable to see the next steps.
I hold tightly onto the fear,
but let excitement
lead me toward you.

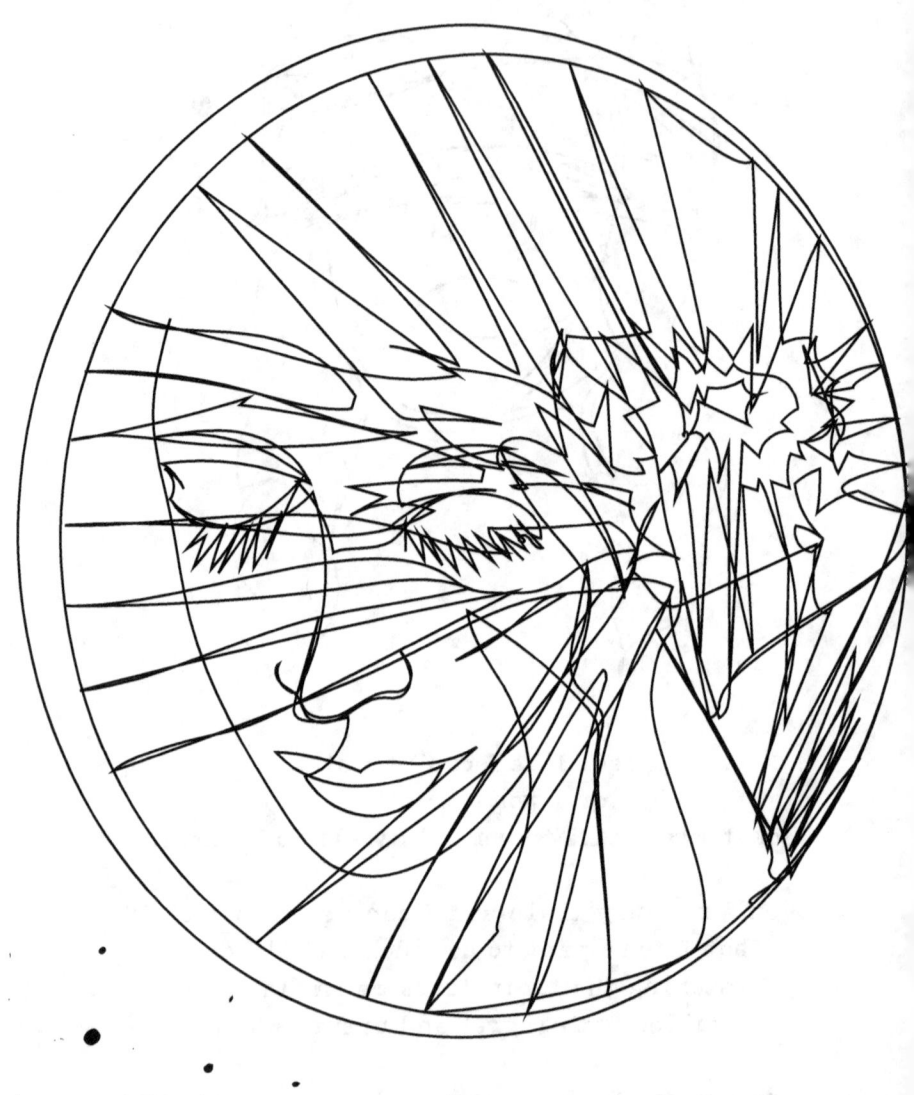

Glass house

The pieces of me scatter across the floor
shimmering like rain.
The jagged edges shards of broken glass.

The face staring back through the pieces broken, too
features no longer line up where they are supposed to.

The eyes that stare back at me seem lost and foreign-
I don't recognize who I've become.

I try to gather the pieces in my hands
to make sense of what I see,
to make sense of what I feel,
but those edges no longer fit together.

A single solitary light shines through
the open window
bouncing off the scattered pieces
so that the room is suddenly dancing in color.

The corners of my mouth turn up slowly
as the light hits my eyes
and I can see what was there all along.

I am not broken.
I never was.

Melting

When our eyes meet,
it feels as though you have always been a part of me.

Your easy, lazy smile ignites a fire inside of me,
warming me from the inside out.

I've always been so cold
before we met,
I didn't realize how much I needed warmth.

Your lips trace scars on my skin,
making me forget they are there at all.

Your kiss makes me dizzy
and excited for the fall.

I can't remember what it was like before you—
before your eyes
or your smile
or your lips
or your kiss.

They fill holes in me I didn't know existed
and now I am full—
whole—
healed.

Your love has helped me see myself as you do,
and together,
we are beautiful.

The list

A *slow dance* in the rain that makes time stand still.

A *soft touch* hiding immeasurable strength within it.

A knowing *smile* that melts my insides and revives me at the same time.

A *glance* from across the room that says so much without a word.

A *hand* on the small of my back guiding me into a room.

A warm bed, tousled sheets, a cool breeze through the open window and *your body* wrapped around mine.

A *whispered word* so only I can hear.

A *kiss* that helps the world make sense and spin out of control all at once.

A *love* that makes me realize what I've been missing and why I've waited so long.

Lost and found

You make me feel
seen,
and *heard,*
and *beautiful,*
and *captivating.*

I never feel lost when you are with me.
In many ways, I think you helped me find myself.
You reminded me
of a beauty and strength and confidence
that was there all along.

You make me
feel,
and *love,*

and *enjoy*
every little thing
and *every little moment.*

I am grateful your path crossed mine,
twisting across one another in the strangest way—
a love I've been searching for without
knowing what I needed to find it.

Fireworks

I want to stand, my back to your chest
underneath explosions of light in the sky
and feel your heartbeat speed up with mine.

I want to lean back to be closer to you
and interlock fingers as you hold my hand.

I want to feel your soft whisper in my ear
as a smile finds its way across my face,
knowing you're wearing one of your own.

I want to feel the tiny sparks that spill across my skin
every time your lips are close.

I want to stand underneath the expanse of sky
and feel that the stars were made for us,
lighting the way as they dance inside your eyes.

I want your mouth to find mine the way that it always does,

*letting our kiss tell our story
better than any words ever will.*

Put me out

A slow burning, like embers smoldering
from a fire dying hours ago-
that is how you leave me.

I am the embers and you are the oxygen
feeding the fire and snuffing it out all at once.

You are like the wind,
blowing softly across my skin
and leaving a trail of sensation in your wake.

I'm standing with my arms wide,
questioning,
wondering,
ready for the embrace,
but unsure of where I'll land.

I try to turn my back to your wind,
but the burning-
that burning leaves clouds of smoke
where you once stood,
and I realize
it's the fire that I really crave.

I keep waiting for the final strike of the match-
waiting for the explosion of fire that follows,
but I wonder if it will light up our worlds
or swallow everything in the flames instead.

Made for you

I am yours and you are mine.
You have my heart-all of it-
just as sure as the blood rushes
through my veins every time
your skin brushes my own.

Your hand grasps tightly to mine
as if you're afraid I may disappear.
But with you, I have no desire to run.
I'm not going anywhere without you beside me.

I think of you and us
in all the small moments throughout the day,
filling empty space and time
with a promised tomorrow
that I impatiently wait for.

And I want it now-
all of it at once-

*the same way
I fell in love with you,*
blindly and without pause.

Full bloom

I remember the moment I knew I loved you,
the exact moment you smiled at me
and my heart exploded in my chest,
planting a million little seeds
that flowered all at once.

That's how it was for me.
It didn't grow slowly the way I expected it to
over a long stretch of time.

It was a simple moment-
just one of so many simple moments
we collect together-
when everything around us came crashing to a halt.

Thoughts of us flew by like a film reel
spinning inexplicably fast
as my heart thudded against my chest
so triumphantly that I swore you could see it.

The realization was dizzying.
It continues to grow unlike everything else in my life
that has always faded to nothing.

I do not know what to do with all this love
and so I shower you with it,
not caring if I give away
every last piece of me in the process.

Balancing Act

When we're together, you light up the entire room.
People take to you immediately while
I try to disappear.
I've never fully been comfortable in the spotlight
but you crave it—beaming when the light shines
brightly on your face.

We both want to be seen,
but you want it from everyone
and all I really want is you.

You are bold and blunt and generally unaffected
while I'm quiet and thoughtful,
usually feeling too much
and needing too much
and never wanting to admit either.

I see and hear while you say—
something that many times keeps us from
being on the same page together,
and yet we continue writing the story
hopeful for the happy ending we both believe in.

Your confidence thrives in different settings than mine,
your skillful hands busy creating
while mine have always been better at fixing,
which is ironic given what we both get paid to do.

Your calm helps quiet the storms inside me
and my blind faith helps you weather any storm.
Our conversations stretch deep—
you longing to be understood
as I live to always know more.

I consume your thoughts and words and dreams,
trying to feed the hunger inside me
that never seems satisfied without learning.

You pace when I remain still.
You push while I retreat.
You believe when I feel lost.

Our love is a beautiful tug of war
that I still don't fully understand
and remain completely in awe of.

Maybe that's all that love is —
a balancing act between two people
who aren't afraid of the fall.

www.ingramcontent.com/pod-product-compliance
Lightning Source LLC
Chambersburg PA
CBHW072210100526
44589CB00015B/2461